Essential Science

Solids & Liquids

Peter Riley

W
FRANKLIN WATTS
LONDON • SYDNEY

First published in 2006 by Franklin Watts
338 Euston Road, London NW1 3BH

Franklin Watts Australia
Hachette Children's Books
Level 17/207 Kent Street, Sydney NSW 2000

Editor: Rachel Tonkin
Designer: Proof Books
Picture researcher: Diana Morris
Illustrations: Ian Thompson

Picture credits:
Kelvin Aitken/Still Pictures: 12b; Jonathan Blair/Corbis: 17t;
Jon Cancalosi/Still Pictures: 15t; Gary W. Carter/Corbis: 14tl,
29tl; Jean-Léo Dugast/Still Pictures: 22c; Simon Fraser/
Science Photo Library: 27; Ingram Publishing/Alamy: 25b;
Mark M. Lawrence/Corbis: 9b; Di Maggio/Still Pictures: 25t;
Gabe Palmer/Corbis: 11t; Fritz Polking/Still Pictures: 13c, 20b;
Secret Sea Visions/Still Pictures: 5cl; Jorgen Schytte/Still
Pictures: 4b; Janine Weidel Photo Library/Alamy: 26t;
Westend61/Alamy: 1, 24b; Michael S. Yamashita/Corbis: 17c.

With thanks to our models: James Cook and Gloria Maddy

A CIP catalogue record for this book
is available from the British Library

ISBN-10: 0 7496 6439 8
ISBN-13: 978 0 7496 6439 8

Dewey Classification: 530.4

Printed in China

CONTENTS

Solids and liquids   4

Volumes   6

Powders   8

Runniness   10

Melting   12

Freezing   14

Separating mixtures of solids   16

When liquids and solids meet   18

Dissolving   20

Separating soluble solids   22

When solids and liquids change   24

New substances   26

Can you remember the essentials?   28

Glossary   30

Answers   31

Index   32

SOLIDS AND LIQUIDS

Everything around you is made up of matter. This is the word scientists use to describe all the substances around us. There are three kinds of matter – solids, liquids and gases. They are known as the three states of matter. In this book we will be looking at two states of matter – solids and liquids.

These wooden blocks are solids. When they are piled up to make a high tower, the block at the bottom holds up the other blocks without being squashed flat.

As solids do not squash easily they can be made to support tall buildings like this one.

Solids keep their shape

A major property of a solid is that it has a fixed shape. If solids did not have a fixed shape how useful would they be? Imagine a wooden chair which changed shape when you sat down on it, or a cup which changed shape when you poured a drink into it. Many solids keep their shape even when there is a weight pressing down on them. They do not squash easily. Can you think of any solids that you can squash. What do you do to flatten them?

Liquids change their shape

The major property of a liquid is that it does not have a fixed shape. When a liquid is poured into a container, it flows and takes the shape of the container. Liquids also cannot be squashed. This means that they can be used for support. Some beds, called waterbeds, have a mattress full of water.

It supports people who sleep on it. Even some worms and slugs have skeletons made from water which support their bodies.

Liquids take up the shape of their containers.

Inside these slugs is a space filled with water. It acts like a skeleton to support the slugs' bodies.

Use the data

When scientists do experiments, they make observations and record them. This information is called data. It may be in a table, bar chart or line graph. Look around you and make a list of all the different solids and liquids you can see and find a total for each. Make them into a bar chart like the one shown here. How does your data compare? Answers to the questions in this book are on page 31.

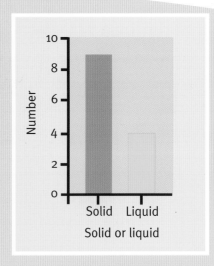

VOLUMES

Everything has a volume. Volume is the amount of space that something takes up and it is measured in cubic centimetres. This is written after the value of the volume as cm³. For example, a volume of 50 cubic centimetres is written as 50 cm³.

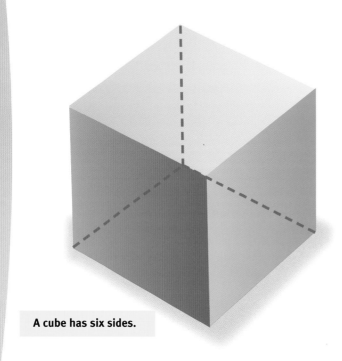

A cube has six sides.

What shape is a cube?

A cube is a shape with six square sides that are all the same size. A dice used for playing many board games is a cube. If each of its edges measures 1cm long it has a volume of one cubic centimetre.

Why scientists measure volume

Scientists measure volume to study the effect of things, such as heat, on different substances. For example, they may need to measure the amount of water produced when a cube of ice melts. Scientists also add liquids to solids or mix liquids together in experiments. To make sure the experiments work, scientists need to measure these volumes.

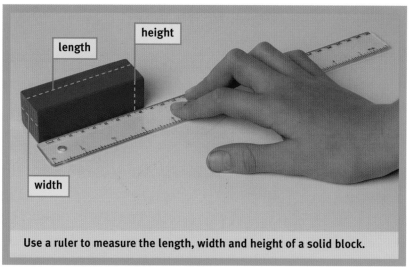

Use a ruler to measure the length, width and height of a solid block.

Finding the volume of a solid block

You can find the volume of a solid block with a ruler. You measure its length, height, width and multiply them together. This block is 9cm long, 3cm high, and 3cm wide. Its volume is 81cm³.

Finding the volume of a liquid

You can find the volume of a liquid by using a beaker or measuring cylinder. There is a scale on the side of the container which measures in millilitres (ml). When you have put a liquid in the container, make sure it is at eye level. You will see the surface of the liquid in the container turns upwards a little when it reaches the sides. You must look at the flat surface of the liquid in the centre of the container to make an accurate measurement.

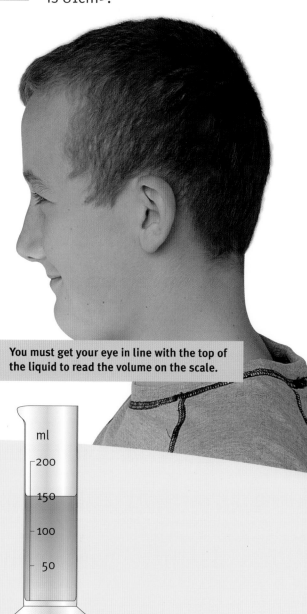

You must get your eye in line with the top of the liquid to read the volume on the scale.

Finding the volumes

1 A wooden block measures 6 cm long, 2 cm high and 4 cm wide. What is its volume?
2 What is the volume of liquid in this measuring cylinder?

POWDERS

Powders are made from very small pieces of solid called particles. The small pieces are made when a larger piece of solid breaks up.

Powdered rock

Over many years the heat of summer and cold of winter break up a rock into grains of sand.

Powders from plants

Grains of wheat contain a white substance which is ground up to make flour. The fruit and seeds of chilli peppers are ground up to make chilli powder.

Are powders like liquids?

Liquids can flow and be poured into a container. When the container is tilted, the liquid keeps a level surface. If a liquid is poured into a sieve it passes straight through. Powders can flow and be poured into a container. If the container is tilted, the powder moves and forms a level surface but it does not do this as quickly or completely as a liquid. Powders can also pass through a sieve but the sieve may have to be tapped a little to help the powder through.

When liquids are poured, they immediately form a flat surface.

Liquids keep a level surface even when you tilt them.

A powder can also be poured, but it forms a cone. The powder will form a level surface if you tilt the plate but not as quickly as a liquid.

Are powders different from liquids?

When a liquid is poured into a container, it forms a flat level surface straight away. If a powder is poured into a container, it forms a cone. If a small amount of a liquid is poured from a jug the liquid falls as drops and a drip forms on the jug's spout. When sand is poured a stream of small grains fall and a drip does not form at the spout.

Powders do not splash and form drops.

The grains in damp sand stick together and can be used to make sand castles.

Powders can stick together

Water makes tiny particles of a solid stick together. Sand is made from tiny particles of rock which behave like a powder.

When they get damp they stick together and can be used to make sandcastles.

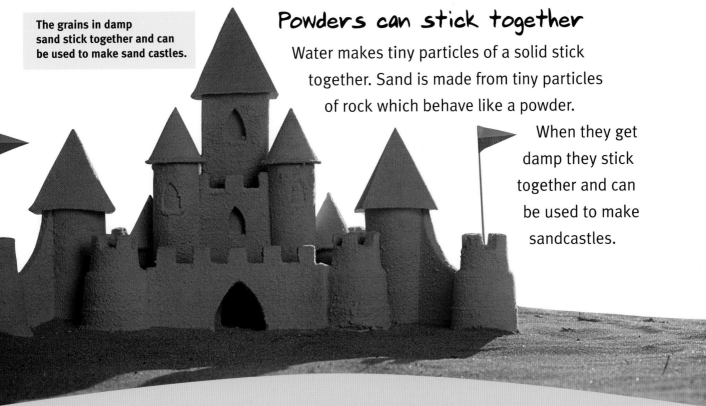

Soil particles

The tiny pieces of solid in a powder are so small that most of them are measured in fractions of a millimetre. Here are four types of tiny pieces found in soil. Arrange them in order starting with the smallest.

Clay	$\frac{1}{500}$ mm
Sand	2 mm
Silt	$\frac{1}{50}$ mm
Grit	$\frac{1}{5}$ mm

RUNNINESS

The runniness of liquids varies depending on what it is. For example, water is much runnier than honey.

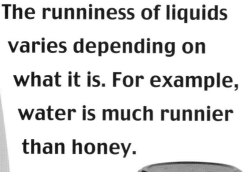

water

honey

cooking oil

foam bath

Testing the runniness of liquids

The runniness of liquids can be compared in the following way. Use a piece of material that does not absorb liquids, such as metal or plastic, to make a slope. Mark a line at the top where the drops of each liquid will be placed and a line at the bottom to show where the timing of the run ends.

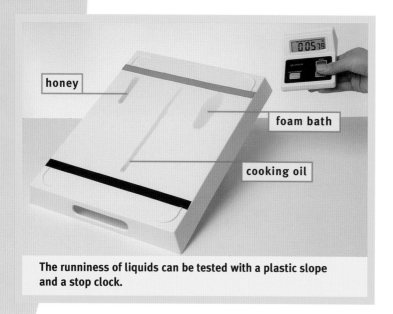

honey

foam bath

cooking oil

The runniness of liquids can be tested with a plastic slope and a stop clock.

As soon as a drop of liquid is placed on the top line, start the stop clock and allow it to run until the liquid reaches the bottom line or until it stops flowing. Write down the time for the run. Test a second drop of liquid on a clean part of the slope. Repeat the test until the runniness of all the liquids has been recorded.

The scientific name for runniness

Scientists use the word viscosity instead of runniness. Viscosity means the 'resistance to flow'. A liquid which flows quickly, such as water, does not have much resistance to flow and is said to have a low viscosity. A liquid which flows very slowly, such as treacle, has a high resistance to flow and is said to have a high viscosity.

Runniness and heat

Liquids which have a high viscosity change when they are heated. Their viscosity becomes lower and they become more runny. Some liquids, such as motor oil, are specially made to run at the high temperatures in an engine. The oil covers the moving metal parts and stops them wearing out as they rub against each other.

A woman checks the amount of oil in her car's engine.

Comparing how liquids run

Here are the times for six liquids to run down a slope.

1 Which liquid had the highest viscosity?

2 Which liquid had the lowest viscosity?

3 Substance F was warmed and then made to run again. Do you think it ran faster or more slowly?

Liquid	Time (seconds)
A	14
B	6
C	10
D	4
E	12
F	7

MELTING

If a solid is heated to a certain temperature, it melts and turns into a liquid.

This chocolate is warmer than its melting point and has turned into a liquid.

What does temperature measure?

The temperature of a substance is a measure of how hot or cold something is. Temperature is measured in °C (Celsius) or °F (Fahrenheit). These are two different scales of temperature.

From solid to liquid

All solids have a fixed shape and most, like metals, have hard surfaces. When they are heated to a certain temperature, the hard surfaces become soft and the fixed shape begins to sag and flatten, and the substance starts to flow. This process of changing from a solid to a liquid is called melting. The temperature at which the solid melts is called the melting point. Different solids melt at different temperatures.

Liquid rock

The inside of the Earth is so hot that it is made up of molten rock. At the surface of the Earth, the rock is cool and forms a thick, solid surface of rock. But at some places on the Earth's surface, the molten rock from inside the Earth breaks through. These are called volcanoes. The hot rock, called magma, behaves just like a liquid and can even form a fountain. It forms a river of molten rock called a lava flow.

The lava from a volcano is molten rock.

Melting polar ice

There are huge sheets of ice at the North and South Poles but changes in the Earth's weather are causing them to melt. As they begin to melt, they break into huge pieces called icebergs, which eventually turn to water and enter the seas and oceans.

As these icebergs melt into the sea they will cause the sea level to rise and some islands to disappear under the water.

Melting points of metals

Here are the melting points of some common metals.

1 Which metal has the highest melting point and which has the lowest?

2 What is the difference in degrees centigrade between the melting point of (a) silver and tin, (b) copper and gold, (c) silver and aluminium?

Metal	Melting point °C
Aluminium	660
Copper	1083
Gold	1064
Iron	1539
Silver	962
Tin	232

FREEZING

Icicles form from drops of water that freeze.

When we think of something freezing we think of water turning to ice, but other substances freeze, too.

Freezing process

If a liquid cools down enough, it stops flowing and takes on a fixed shape. The liquid has turned into a solid in a process called freezing. The temperature at which this change takes place is called the freezing point. The freezing point of a substance is the same as its melting point.

Candle wax and lava

When a candle is lit, a pool of wax forms at the top below the flame. If too much wax melts, it flows down the side of the candle. As the molten wax moves away from the warm top of the candle, it cools until its freezing point is reached then turns into a solid.

Lava freezes in a similar way to wax. It flows from the volcano until it reaches its freezing point and then turns into rock. Large drops of molten rock, which fly through the air from a lava fountain, turn to rock as they reach their freezing point and fall as rocky lumps called volcanic bombs.

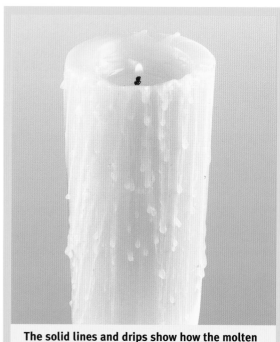

The solid lines and drips show how the molten wax flowed down the candle before it froze.

When this metal freezes it takes the shape of the mould.

Powders from frozen solids

Clouds are made from tiny water drops which collect together. At the top of the cloud it is so cold that the water drops freeze and form ice crystals. Normally these fall as rain, but in cold weather they remain frozen and fall to the ground and make powdery snow.

Casting metals

When a metal is cast it is heated until it melts and then poured into a mould. The liquid metal takes up the shape of the mould, then cools and freezes. A mould is used to make the metal into complicated shapes, such as a car engine.

Freezing points

Here are the freezing points of six substances.

1 If the temperature fell from 30°C to -10°C what is the order in which the substances would freeze?

2 Which substances would still be liquids at (a) 20°C and (b) 10°C?

Substance	Freezing point °C
A	11
B	25
C	17
D	−5
E	27
F	4

SEPARATING MIXTURES OF SOLIDS

Very small pieces of solids are called particles. If the particles are different sizes they can be separated by sieving.

How does a sieve work?

A sieve is made from a wire gauze or mesh. If the holes in it are larger than some particles but smaller than others, the sieve can separate them. The particles that are smaller than the holes pass through them, while the particles that are larger are held back in the sieve.

Sieving in the kitchen

When salt or sugar gets damp, large lumps can form. The mixture of lumps and salt or sugar grains can be separated by pouring it into a sieve then gently shaking it.

Sieving in the garden

Garden soil can have rocks and broken bricks in it. These can get in the way of the plant roots and stop them growing properly. The rocks and bricks can be removed by placing the soil in a large sieve called a riddle. This has holes in it which are large enough to let soil particles pass through but small enough to hold back stones and pieces of brick.

When lumpy sugar is sieved, the small grains fall through the holes but the lumps remain behind.

Sieving on a dig

When archaeologists take up the soil at a dig, they shake it on a big sieve. Small particles of soil pass through but larger items such as pins, coins and pieces of pottery do not. They are collected and examined by the archaeologists to help find out about people who lived in the past.

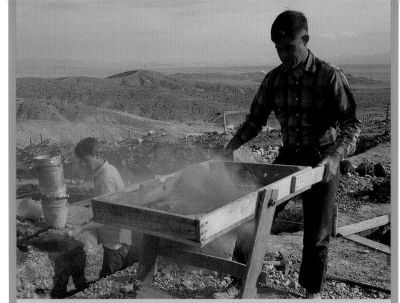

This sieve is being shaken to separate the soil from items such as ancient pottery.

In some places, sieving flour is still done by hand.

Sieving at a flour mill

When wheat grains are ground up to make white flour, the powder in the grains is separated from other parts of the grain by sieving.

Sieves and particles

The table shows the size of particles in three different solids

Solid	Particle size (mm)
A	3
B	2
C	1

There are two sieves available:
X has holes which are 2.5 mm wide and
Y has holes which are 1.5 mm wide.

1 If a mixture contained particles of all three solids what would happen when you used (a) sieve X to separate them, (b) sieve Y to separate them?

2 How could you use the sieves to separate the particles of the three solids?

WHEN LIQUIDS AND SOLIDS MEET

When solids and liquids meet, the liquids flow around the solids and the solids may float, sink or dissolve.

Dissolving solids

Solids that dissolve are called soluble solids. You can read about them on pages 20—21. These two pages are about solids that do not dissolve, called insoluble solids.

Floating solids

All solids have weight, which is a force that pushes downwards. All liquids push upwards on solids with a force called the upthrust. If the weight of a solid pushing down on the liquids is less than the upthrust, the solid floats on the liquid.

grass

clay particles form a suspension

sand and grit form a sediment

Soil is a mixture of solid particles which have different weights.

Sinking solids

If the weight of the solid is more than the upthrust, the solid sinks. But its sinking speed depends on a force called water resistance. Large solids have less water resistance than small objects and so sink faster. Tiny particles sink very slowly and form a suspension.

Sediments

Large solids sink to the bottom of the liquid straight away. They form a layer called a sediment. If a mixture of solids of different sizes is mixed with a liquid, the solids with the greatest size sink first and the solids with the smallest size sink last.

Filtering

Mixtures of insoluble solids and liquids can be separated by filtering. A filter is made from filter paper. Filter paper has tiny holes in it which lets the liquid flow through it but holds back particles of insoluble solids. The filter is made by folding the paper into a cone then turning it upside down in a filter funnel.

filter

sand

water

The water passes through the filter paper but the sand is held back.

water

gauze

ground coffee

When the plunger is pushed down in the cafetière, the water flows up through the gauze but the ground coffee beans are pushed to the bottom.

Filtering coffee

Coffee made in a cafetière is filtered when the plunger is pushed down. The plunger has a gauze which is similar to filter paper.

How do they sink?

Four solids with particles of different sizes are mixed with water. All have weights which are larger than the upthurst. What is the order in which they form a sediment?

Solid	Particle size (mm)
A	40
B	1
C	10
D	5

DISSOLVING

If certain solids and liquids are mixed together, the solid seems to disappear into the liquid. When this happens we say that the solid has dissolved in the liquid. Solids that dissolve are called soluble solids.

What happens to the solid?

When a solid dissolves, it breaks up into very tiny pieces, called particles, which are so small that they cannot be seen. The particles of some solids, such as instant coffee granules, give the liquid a colour but the particles of others, such as salt and sugar, do not.

Sugar cubes begin to dissolve when they are left in water.

Water flowing through this rock has dissolved parts of it away to make a cave.

Some dissolved particles, such as those of salt and sugar, give the liquid a particular taste but the particles of rocks found in mineral waters do not. A liquid with a solid dissolved in it is called a solution.

Speeding up dissolving

Breaking up

When a solid dissolves, tiny particles of it escape at its surface and enter the liquid. A big lump of a solid looks as if it has a large surface but if it is broken down into smaller bits, their surfaces are even greater. This allows more particles to escape into the liquid and speeds up dissolving.

Stirring up

If the water around the bits of solid is still, the particles move into it quickly at first but as they start to fill it up they move more slowly. When the water is stirred, it flows over the bits, picks up particles and moves on. Every second a new portion of water sweeps by the bits and takes away the particles so it continues to dissolve quickly.

Stirring up coffee granules help them dissolve into the water.

Heating up

When solids warm up, the tiny particles in them shake about very slightly. If the solid is in a liquid the particles at its surface shoot off quickly into the liquid and dissolve. The hotter the solid and liquid the faster the solid dissolves.

Solubility

The solubility of a solid is found by measuring the mass of it that will dissolve in 100 cm^3 of water. The higher the mass that dissolves, the higher the solubility. The mass is measured in grammes (g).

1 Which solid is the most soluble?

2 Which solid is the least soluble?

3 (a) Is D more soluble than A?

  (b) Is C more soluble than B?

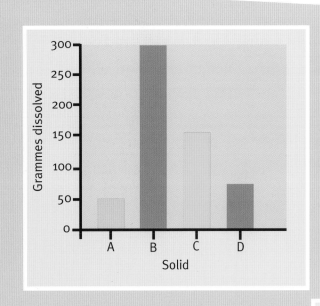

SEPARATING SOLUBLE SOLIDS

The particles of a dissolved solid can be separated from liquid by evaporation or chromatography, a technique used to separate substances.

Going through the holes

A filter paper cannot be used to separate a liquid from the solid particles dissolved in it. The particles are smaller than the holes in the paper and pass through them with the liquid.

Evaporation

Tiny particles break off from the surface of a liquid and form a gas (see page 24). The gas spreads out and mixes with the air. This process is called evaporation. Evaporation takes place at the normal temperatures around us. A liquid will keep on evaporating until all of it has turned into a gas. We say the liquid has dried up.

Sea water contains large amounts of dissolved salt. When it is placed in shallow pans and allowed to evaporate, the salt is left behind. These women are collecting the salt.

Leaving the solid behind

Solids cannot evaporate. If a solid is dissolved in a liquid its particles stay behind while liquid particles evaporate. Eventually there is not enough liquid around the solid particles to keep them dissolved so they turn back into a solid again.

Chromatography

Chromatography can be used to separate a number of different soluble solids from their solution. A filter paper is used, not to filter the solution but to carry it along. As the liquid moves up through the filter paper, the solids which do not dissolve very well settle out on the paper first and the solids that dissolve very well settle out last. If the solids are different coloured dyes, they form coloured patches as they settle out.

The different dyes in the ink settle out on the paper, showing the colours mixed to make the ink.

Time to evaporate

Some water was put into saucers and left to evaporate at different temperatures.

1 What happens to the way water evaporates as it gets warmer?

2 If you wanted to make the water evaporate more quickly than three days what should you do?

Temperature (°C)	Evaporation time (days)
5	12
10	9
15	6
20	3

WHEN SOLIDS AND LIQUIDS CHANGE

Solids and liquids take part in two kinds of changes. These are called reversible and irreversible changes.

Reversible changes

When a solid is heated it melts and turns into a liquid. This change is reversible because when the liquid cools down, it freezes and turns back into a solid.

As the water boils it changes into a gas.

What we often think is steam coming from a hot drink is actually condensed water droplets.

When water evaporates it forms a gas called water vapour. This change is reversed when the water vapour changes back into a liquid again in a process called condensation.

When a liquid is heated very strongly, bubbles form in it and rise to its surface. The hot bubbling liquid is said to be boiling. The temperature at which a liquid boils is called its boiling point. As a liquid boils it changes into a gas. Boiling is reversed when the gas cools down and changes back into a liquid by condensation.

Irreversible changes

If a solid such as wood is heated very strongly it burns. During the burning process, flames rise from the wood and it changes into a substance called ash. Some of the wood turns into particles which rise in the air and make smoke. A substance in the wood, called carbon, takes part in a change with a gas in the air called oxygen. They make a new gas called carbon dioxide. If ash, smoke and carbon dioxide are put together they do not make wood again. This is why burning is an irreversible change.

The burning wood gives out light and heat.

Egg white takes part in an irreversible change when it is heated.

When some substances get hot they do not burn but change in another way. Egg white is a clear liquid but when it is heated in a pan it becomes cloudy then white and changes into a solid.

The three states of zinc

Here are the melting and boiling points of a metal called zinc. It is used to make buckets and battery cases.

Zinc has a melting point of 420°C and a boiling point of 788°C.

Imagine the zinc at each of these temperatures:

A 20 °C; **B** 801°C; **C** 500°C

At which temperature was zinc
(a) a solid, **(b)** a liquid, **(c)** a gas?

NEW SUBSTANCES

When an irreversible change takes place, a new material is formed. The new material has different properties from the substances it is made from. Many materials we use are made this way.

The clay sets hard when it is heated strongly.

Pottery

Clay is a soft solid that can be squashed and pressed to make many kinds of shapes. When it is put in a kiln and heated to over 800°C, it sets hard to form pottery. The shape of a piece of pottery cannot be changed. If it falls on the floor it does not just flatten like clay, but shatters into many pieces. We use pottery for cups, bowls, plates and jars.

Concrete

Cement is a powder used to make concrete. It is mixed with water and other substances and can be poured where it is needed. It sets to make concrete which cannot be changed.

Concrete is made in a concrete mixer and then poured out where it is needed.

Plaster of Paris

If a person has a broken arm or leg, it is treated by covering it in bandage coated in plaster of Paris. Plaster of Paris is a white powder but when water is added to it a creamy mixture forms then sets into a hard, white solid. If you could look at the solid with a microscope, you would see that the tiny fragments of powder had formed crystals which locked together like the pieces in a jigsaw to make the new substance hard.

Plastic

The plastics that we use today are made from substances in oil and natural gas. One substance is called ethene. It is a gas but when it is heated strongly and squashed it changes into a new solid substance that scientists called polyethene. Most people call it polythene. It is used to make bags, bottle and bowls.

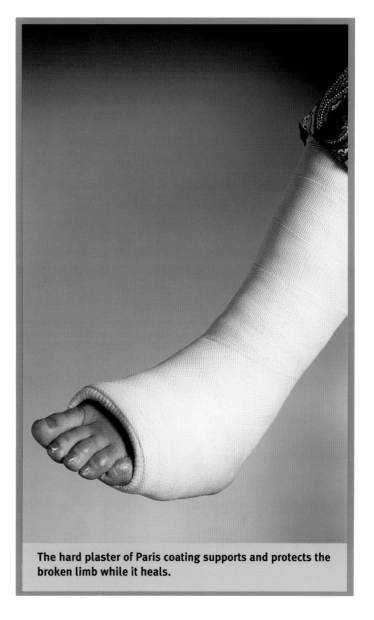

The hard plaster of Paris coating supports and protects the broken limb while it heals.

Reversible and irreversible changes

Here are some observations on changes.
Which changes have formed a new substance?

A. Hot dough turns into bread
B. Warm butter turns into a liquid.
C. Slices of bread get a brown coating in a toaster.

CAN YOU REMEMBER THE ESSENTIALS?

Here are the essential science facts about solids and liquids. They are set out in the order you can read about them in the book. Spend a couple of minutes learning each set of facts. If you can learn them all, you know all the essentials about two states of matter — solids and liquids.

Volumes (pages 6-7)
The volume is the amount of space that a thing takes up.
Volumes are measured in cubic centimetres (cm^3).
A beaker or measuring cylinder is used to measure the volume of a liquid.
The volume of a block can be found by measuring its length, height and width with a ruler and multiplying them all together.

Runniness (pages 10-11)
The runniness of a liquid can be tested by timing how long it takes to run down a slope.
The scientific word for runniness is viscosity.
A liquid with a low viscosity runs quickly.
A liquid with a high viscosity runs slowly.
When a liquid is heated its viscosity becomes lower.

Powders (pages 8-9)
A powder is made from very small pieces of solid.
Very small pieces of a solid are called particles.
Sand and flour behave like powders.
Powders can be poured.
Powders do not form drops.
Powders do not spread out when poured but form a cone.

Melting (pages 12-13)
If a solid is heated strongly enough it melts.
A solid turns into a liquid when it melts.
The temperature at which a solid melts is called its melting point.

Freezing (pages 14-15)

If a liquid is cooled down enough it freezes.
When a liquid freezes it turns into a solid.
The temperature at which a liquid freezes is called its freezing point.
The freezing point is the same as the melting point.

Dissolving (pages 20-21)

Solids which dissolve in a liquid are called soluble solids.
A liquid with a solid dissolved in it is called a solution.
Soluble solids can give a solution a colour and a taste.
The very tiny pieces of solid that dissolve are called particles. Remember that this word is also used for small pieces of solids too, such as grains of sand.
Dissolving can be speeded up by breaking up the solid into small pieces, stirring or warming the liquid.

Separating mixtures of solids (pages 16-17)

A sieve has holes in it.
A sieve can be used to separate solids which have particles of different sizes.
Small particles pass through the holes in a sieve.
Large particles cannot pass through the holes in a sieve.

Separating soluble solids (pages 22-23)

Particles of a dissolved solid can be separated from a liquid by evaporation.
When a liquid evaporates it turns into a gas.
Solids cannot evaporate.
In chromatography, solid particles settle out on a filter paper as the liquid soaks through it.

When liquids and solids meet (pages 18-19)

Solids which dissolve in a liquid are said to be soluble. Solids which do not dissolve in a liquid are said to be insoluble.

When insoluble solids mix with a liquid, they may float, form a suspension or a sediment.
Insoluble solids can be separated from a liquid by filtering.

When solids and liquids change (pages 24-25)

If a substance takes part in a reversible change it can be changed back again.
Melting, freezing, evaporating and condensing, boiling and condensing are reversible changes.
The temperature at which a liquid boils is called its boiling point.
If a substance takes part in an irreversible change it cannot be changed back again.
Irreversible changes take place when a substance burns or is cooked.

New substances (pages 26-27)

A new substance is made when an irreversible change takes place.
The new substance has different properties to the substances that took part in the irreversible change.

GLOSSARY

Archaeologist A person who studies the the past by examining the things people made and used.

Chemical reaction A change that takes place between two or more substances which cannot be reversed.

Chromatography The separation of coloured substances dissolved in a liquid by allowing them to flow through paper with small holes in it.

Condensation A process in which a gas turns into a liquid when it cools.

Crystals Solids with a number of flat sides which are arranged at certain angles to each other.

Dissolve A process in which a substance separates and spreads out through a liquid and seems to disappear into it.

Evaporation A process in which a liquid changes into a gas at a temperature below the boiling point of the liquid.

Freezing A process in which a liquid changes into a solid.

Freezing point The temperature at which a liquid changes into a solid.

Gases Substances which do not have any certain shape or volume.

Irreversible change A change which takes place in a substance that cannot be reversed by a simple process such as melting or freezing.

Insoluble solids Solids which will not dissolve in a liquid.

Melting A process in which a solid changes into a liquid.

Melting point The temperature at which a solid melts and changes into a liquid.

Metal A shiny solid, usually hard which conducts both heat and electricity well.

Plastic A solid material made from substances in oil and gas which can be heated and moulded into many shapes.

Property A special feature that a material possesses such as having a high viscosity or a low melting point.

Reversible change A change which can be reversed. For example, melting is reversed by freezing and evaporating is reversed by condensing.

Sediment The layer of insoluble solids that settle out at the bottom of a liquid when the liquid and the solids have been mixed together.

Soluble solids Solids which dissolve in a liquid.

Solubility The amount of a substance that will dissolve in a certain amount of a liquid.

Solution A liquid in which a substance has dissolved.

Suspension A large number of tiny solid particles which appear to float in a liquid but are actually slowly sinking.

Temperature The measure of the hotness or coldness of a substance.

Upthrust The force of a liquid pushing upwards on an object that has entered it.

Viscosity The property of a liquid concerned with how fast it flows. A liquid with a high viscosity flows slowly, a liquid with a low viscosity flows quickly.

Weight The force of an object pressing down towards the centre of the earth.

ANSWERS

Volumes (pages 6–7)
1 48 cm^3
2 150ml

Powders (pages 8–9)
Clay, silt, grit, sand.

Runniness (pages 10–11)
1 A
2 D
3 It ran faster.

Melting (page 12–13)
1 Iron, tin.
2 (a) 730 °C, (b) 19°C, (c) 302°C.

Freezing (pages 14–15)
1 E, B, C, A, F, D.
2 (a) A, C, D, F (b) D, F.

Separating mixtures of solids (Page 16–17)
1 (a) Solids B and C would pass through Sieve X and Solid A would be left in the sieve (b) Solid C would pass through Sieve Y but solids A and B would be left in the sieve.
2 Use sieve X to separate A from B and C, then use sieve Y to separate B and C.

When solids an liquids meet (pages 18–19)
A sinks first then C, D and B.

Dissolving (Page 20–21)
1 B
2 A
3 (a) Yes, (b) No.

Separating soluble solids (Page 22–23
1 As it gets warmer the water evaporates faster.
2 Put it somewhere warmer than 20 °C.

When solids and liquids change (Page 24–25)
(a) A
(b) C
(c) B

New substances (page 26–27)
A and B

INDEX

aluminium 13

boiling 24, 25
   point 24, 25

carbon 25
   dioxide 25
Celsius 12
centigrade 13
change
   irreversible 24, 25, 26,
   27, 29
   reversible 24, 27, 29
chemical reaction 6
chromatography 22, 23, 29
clay 9, 18, 26
condensation 24
copper 13
crystals 9, 15, 27
cubic centimetres (cm3) 6,
   7, 28

data 4
dice 6
dissolving 18, 20, 21, 22,
   23, 29
dye 23

ethene 27
evaporation 22, 23, 24,
   29
explosion 6

Fahrenheit 12
filter 19, 29
   paper 19, 22, 23
fixed shape 4, 5, 12, 14
flour 8, 17
freezing 14, 24, 29
   point 14, 15, 29

gas 4, 22, 24, 25, 27, 29
gold 13
grammes (g) 21
grit 9, 18

heat 8, 11, 12, 15, 21,
   24, 25, 26, 27, 28
height 7, 28

ice 14
icebergs 13
insoluble solids 18, 19, 29
iron 13
irreversible change 24, 25,
   26, 27, 29

lava 12, 14, 15
   flow 12
   fountain 12, 14
length 7, 28
liquids 4, 5, 6, 7, 8, 9, 10,
   11, 12, 14, 15, 18, 19, 20,
   21, 22, 23, 24, 25, 27, 28
   flow of 10, 11, 14

magma 12
mass 21
matter 4, 28
measuring cylinder 7, 28
melting 12, 13, 24, 25, 28
   point 12, 13, 14, 25,
   28, 29
metal 10, 11, 12, 13, 15, 25
millimetre 9

North Pole 13

oil 10, 11, 27
oxygen 25

particles 8, 9, 16, 17,
   18, 19, 20, 21, 22,
   25, 28, 29
   of salt 9
   of soil 9
plaster of Paris 27
plastic 10, 27
polyethene 27
powder 8, 9, 26, 27, 28
property 4, 5, 29

reversible change 24, 27, 29
rock 8, 16, 20
   molten 12, 14
   powdered 8
runniness 10, 11, 28

salt 9, 16, 20, 22
sand 8, 9, 15, 18, 19, 29
sediment 18, 19, 29
sieve 8, 16, 29
silt 9
silver 13
soil 9, 16, 17, 18
solids 4, 5, 6, 7, 8, 12, 14, 16,
   17, 18, 20, 21, 22, 23, 24,
   25, 26, 27, 28, 29
   insoluble 18, 19, 29
   soluble 18, 20, 21, 23, 29
soluble solids 18, 20, 21, 23,
   29
solution 20, 29
South Pole 13
suspension 18, 29

temperature 11, 12, 14, 15,
   23, 25, 28, 29
tin 13

upthrust 18, 19

viscosity 11, 28
volcano 12, 14
volume 6, 7, 28

water 5, 10, 11, 13, 14, 18, 19,
   20, 21, 22, 23, 24, 26, 27
   droplets 15
   vapour 24
waterbed 5
weather 13, 15
weight 4, 18, 19
wheat 8, 17
width 7, 28

zinc 25